They Lied About SEO

What Google Won't Tell You About
Getting Found Without Ads

Eric F Gilbert

ISBN: 978-1-968365-02-8

Dedication

To the underdogs.

Those who started their business from
nothing, earned every sale, and stayed
committed regardless of recognition.
You don't need permission—you just
need the right strategy.

This book is for you.

About the Author

Eric F Gilbert is a nationally recognized entrepreneur, marketing strategist, and author of multiple business books, including *Broke to Business Boss* and *5 Secrets Millionaires Don't Want You to Know*. With over 25 years of experience building companies and getting them seen, Eric has helped hundreds of small business owners dominate their industries—without breaking the bank. He doesn't chase algorithms. He teaches people how to become the algorithm.

Table of Contents

Introduction: Why You're Still Invisible

Most SEO agencies are not going to tell you that you can do what you need to get found online by yourself. I'm not saying it's easy—but it's true. And it's not expensive.

That's what they're not telling you. You don't need fancy tricks or fancy coding—just discipline and steady work. In this book, I'll show you what I've learned from working inside big fancy agencies, and from doing this by myself for years.

Here's the hard truth: most of what you've been told about search engine optimization is outdated, overpriced, or deliberately confusing. That's not an accident. Agencies make money by making SEO sound technical and mysterious. They want you to feel like you need them. And for a long time, people believed that—because for a while, code did matter more.

But that world has changed.

Search engines today don't care as much about your meta tags or your bounce rate. They care about what people are saying. What they're clicking. What gets shared, saved, reviewed, and mentioned. They care about you being visible in the right conversations.

And if you understand that, you can work with the system instead of being held hostage by it.

That's what this book is about. I'm not here to teach you code. I'm here to teach you visibility. Real visibility—the kind that gets you found when people ask Siri a question or scroll TikTok for answers. I'll walk you through how search engines really think, why old tactics don't work anymore, and how to legally dominate the digital space with strategy, not budget.

This book is for the hustlers, the small business owners, the side giggers, the underdogs. If you've got something worth being found, I'll show you how to make it visible.

Let's get started.

Chapter 1: The Roots of SEO – Black Hat, White Hat, and the Gray in Between

If you want to understand how to win at visibility today, you've got to understand how this whole game started. SEO didn't begin as a polished strategy—it started as a hack. A workaround. A way to manipulate early search engines into putting your site at the top.

In the beginning, it was the Wild West.

All you had to do was stuff your page full of keywords. Want to rank for "real estate Florida"? You'd just copy-paste that phrase 500 times on a white background, in white font, at the bottom of your website. The search engine crawlers would read it, but your visitors wouldn't see it. That was called black hat SEO—a term borrowed from old cowboy movies where the villain always wore black.

Black hat strategies were all about tricking the system: hidden text, cloaking, doorway pages, paid link schemes, blog comment spam. It worked, for a while. Some people got rich off it.

I knew a guy that had literal "farms" of websites running on his own servers. Just dummy sites—hundreds of them—that didn't serve a real purpose except to point backlinks at whatever client site he was trying to boost. One guy I knew had over 500 sites sitting on a single server in his office alone. None of them had real traffic. None of them offered value. But they worked—until they didn't.

Then Google started fighting back.

Each time a new exploit got too popular, Google rolled out an update to kill it. Panda crushed content farms. Penguin penalized spammy links. Hummingbird shifted the game from matching keywords to understanding meaning. BERT brought in natural language processing. And now? Google's AI models are analyzing your site the same way a human would. If it doesn't sound real or relevant, you're done.

That's when white hat SEO started to rise—strategies that played by the rules. Focus on quality content. Build backlinks naturally. Speed up your site. Use descriptive titles and alt text. Make sure your site is mobile-friendly. Nothing wrong with that advice. In fact, most of it still matters—but not for the reasons people think.

Here's what the SEO industry doesn't want to admit: most of these "white hat" methods are just the new version of old tricks. They might not get you penalized, but they also don't guarantee results. And most business owners don't have the time to chase every Google guideline or Core Web Vital change.

So they hire SEO agencies.

And at first, it looks like it's working. Rankings go up. Traffic spikes. The agency sends reports with charts and color-coded improvements. But then? Google updates the algorithm again— and the rankings drop. The traffic slows. And you're left wondering what just happened.

Here's the truth: most SEO companies are selling band-aids, not strategy. They're not building real visibility— they're building temporary compliance. And compliance only lasts until the next rule change.

That's why black hat doesn't work long-term. It's why white hat doesn't always work either. And it's why I operate in what I call the gray zone—not shady, but smart. I don't try to trick the algorithm. I work with it. I understand what it's looking for now—and more importantly, what it's likely to favor next.

Because let's be real: Google's not the only game in town anymore. Bing is buying search results from third-party sources. Yahoo runs on Bing. Even DuckDuckGo pulls from other indexes. Most of them are copying Google—or outright paying to use its model.

As of this writing, over 92% of global searches still go through Google. Bing accounts for roughly 3%, and Yahoo less than 1%. Even newer tools like Brave Search and You.com rely on hybrid results. In short: follow Google, and you're covered everywhere else too.

And now we've got voice search—Siri, Alexa, Google Assistant. Guess what they do? They pick the most trusted, visible, conversationally relevant answer. You don't rank in voice search by stuffing keywords or fixing your site speed. You rank by being the most talked about.

That's what this book is here to teach you.

In the chapters ahead, I'll break down exactly what the search engines are looking for—not in theory, but in practice. I'll show you how to saturate your niche with content, comments, mentions, and reviews. I'll show you how to show up in places the algorithm already trusts. And I'll show you how to dominate digital space without getting penalized, paying for ads, or depending on someone else's platform.

One last dirty detail about what Google sees when they look at your site's links and keywords. When they are about to serve up a search result, and they look at your site, if your site has all the perfect keywords, and all of the perfect backlinks, and an article that seems to address the question in search, they may return your site. However, if Google finds a site that has a more "raw" site that is talked about more in social media, has more relevant articles, the articles are written in a more helpful way, no keyword stuffing on your site, only real backlinks to your site, you can bet which site Google is going to return every single time now that Google is reading the site with ai.

reading the site with ai.

Chapter 2: What Search Engines Actually Want

Let's set the record straight—search engines don't care about your business.

Google doesn't wake up in the morning wondering how to get you more traffic. Bing isn't pulling for your brand. Yahoo isn't trying to help you get sales. These platforms don't care who you are, they care whether you look like the best answer for the person doing the search.

That's it. That's the whole game.

Search engines are in the customer satisfaction business, not the SEO business. Their #1 job is to give users the most relevant, trustworthy, and useful result as fast as possible. And that means they're constantly analyzing what people click on, what they stay on, and what they trust.

So, while most business owners are out here obsessing over keyword density or site speed, the real winners are the ones who understand what these platforms are really measuring: **authority**, **context**, and **intent**.

---

1. Authority: Who's Talking About You?

Search engines aren't just looking at your site. They're scanning everything around it. Are other-trusted sources mentioning you? Are people linking to your content organically? Are customers leaving real reviews? Are your videos being shared, tagged, quoted?

That's authority. And it doesn't have to come from CNN or Forbes. It can come from niche blogs, local news, Reddit threads, YouTube comments, or podcast mentions. The more your name appears in trusted digital spaces, the more you rise in the algorithm's eyes.

Authority is built through presence—not perfection.

---

2. Context: What Do You Seem to Be About?

Back in the old days, if you wanted to rank for "plumber Tampa," you just shoved those words all over your site. That doesn't work anymore. Google's AI is smart enough to read your page like a human would. It knows if your content actually talks about plumbing, or if you're just stuffing the words in.

Even more than that, it reads your surrounding signals. What do other sites that link to you talk about? What does your Google Business profile say? What do your customers say in reviews? What kinds of posts show up when people Google your name or brand?

That's why search engines now use **entity-based indexing**. They're not ranking pages based on keywords, they're ranking **entities** based on trust, clarity, and topic alignment. You don't just want to be a plumber in Tampa. You want to be the most visible, most relevant **plumbing-related entity** in that region.

3. Intent: Are You the Answer to the Question?

This one is huge. Modern search engines don't just look at the words in a search—they try to figure out what the person actually wants.

If someone types "how to fix a clogged sink," Google doesn't show a homepage for a plumbing company. It shows a blog post or YouTube video that directly answers that question.

If someone searches "best coffee near me," it's not giving them the site with the most backlinks. It's showing the place with good reviews, recent check-ins, and photos that match what people expect from a good coffee spot.

In other words, the algorithm is trying to match **search intent** with **conversation patterns**. It's looking at what similar people clicked on, what kind of content they stuck with, and what other sources are saying about the results.

So, What Does This Mean for You?

It means you don't need to obsess over coding tricks. You need to show up in the right places, in the right way, with the right kind of content. And you need to do it consistently enough that Google starts to see you as a pattern—not just a page.

And here's the kicker: this applies to all the search engines.

Google may be the biggest, but almost every other platform is either copying it—or literally buying its results.

Google controls about 92% of the global search market. Bing holds about 3%, and Yahoo around 1%. Most smaller engines either license their results from Bing (which is itself trying to copy Google) or blend them with public indexes. Even DuckDuckGo pulls from Bing and other partners.

That means if you optimize for Google the right way, you're automatically optimized for everything else.

Even Alexa, Siri, and Google Assistant rely on a form of algorithmic summarization based on search signals—not "rankings." When someone asks, "What's the best vegan restaurant in Atlanta?" the smart assistant isn't reading ten blue links. It's picking the one most relevant, trustworthy, and well-connected answer.

Chapter 3: Gaming the System – How Search Really Works

Most people think that to get found online, it's all about how your website is built and how much you spend on ads.

What if I told you that's nowhere near the truth?

Sure, your website structure matters a little. But if you want to dominate search results, if you want to own the space when someone types in something related to your business—you have to understand what search engines are really looking for.

And it starts way before someone ever types a word into a search bar.

Search Doesn't Start With Search.

Search starts with conversation. With behavior. With data, your data, and the data of everyone around you.

When you create an email account... when you text your friend about trying a new diet... when you like a post about Cancun on Instagram... when your buddy DMs you a TikTok about golf swings... that's when search actually begins.

Not when you Google something. Not when you open Safari or click a link.

By the time you "search," the algorithm already knows what it thinks you're looking for.

The System is Always Listening.

Literally.

Your phone is listening. Your smart speaker is listening. Your apps are tracking you—not just where you go, but what you say. If you talk about golf clubs while you're driving, you'll probably see ads for Callaway drivers before you even get home.

That's not coincidence. That's algorithmic targeting.

And it's not just you. It's your circle.

Search engines and ad networks also look at what your friends are clicking. What they buy. What they've searched. Who they follow. What content they interact with. If five of your contacts suddenly become obsessed with a new energy drink, guess what's going to show up in your YouTube ads tomorrow?

The algorithm assumes you're part of a pattern. And it acts on that assumption constantly.

Search Engines Are Data Interpreters Now.

They're not ranking websites—they're ranking conversations.

They're tracking:

- What you read

- What you like

- What you watch

- What you replay

- What you talk about—even when you don't type it

That's why so many people feel like their phones are "reading their minds." They're not. They're just insanely good at predicting your interests based on behavior clusters.

This is the foundation of Google's algorithm now. Same with Facebook, Amazon, TikTok, Alexa, Siri—you name it.

They don't wait for you to ask the question anymore. They push the content they think you're most likely to engage with based on everything you've already done.

So How Do You Use This to Your Advantage?

Simple: if the system is listening for conversations, you need to be in the conversation.

That's where your energy should go.

- Share content that's keyword-rich but sounds natural

- Get other people to tag, share, and quote you

- Start conversations—and join existing ones

- Get mentioned on podcasts, in blog posts, in forums

- Build a presence that feels like a pattern

Search engines reward patterns. The more your name pops up in different platforms, in different contexts, but always pointing back to the same core idea—you get elevated.

People Think SEO is About Code. It's Not.

It's about conversation.
It's about saturation.

Let me break it down in high school terms: there are two ways to get popular. You can become the quarterback—or you can get the whole band to say you're cool. The second one is easier. And it works the same online.

Let's say your competitor ranks #1 on Google. You might think that means they're winning.

But I can teach you how to cover the next five pages of Google results with articles, blog posts, press mentions, videos, and social proof.

Who do you think gets more traffic—the guy with one link in the #1 spot, or the one whose name keeps showing up on page after page?

In a Voice-First World, Conversation is Everything

Even more important: smart devices only give one answer.

When you ask Siri or Alexa, "What's the best bakery near me?" it's not pulling from just search rank. It's pulling from conversational authority—from whoever looks most relevant in social signals, data trends, and topic clustering.

That's why the old SEO tricks are dying.

You can't game voice search with keyword stuffing. You can't rank on Siri by having a nice site. You rank by being the most talked about, recommended, searched, and clicked.

This Isn't Black Hat. It's Just Smart.

And here's the part most agencies won't tell you: this strategy? It's 100% legal. It's not a trick. It's not black hat SEO. It's exactly what the algorithm wants.

It's just not what marketing firms sell you—because most of them don't know how to do it. And even if they do, they don't know how to charge you for it.

That's where this book comes in.

I'm not going to teach you how to code. I'm going to teach you how to be everywhere—how to make yourself, your brand, or your product so present in the right kinds of conversations that the internet starts working for you instead of against you.

This is how I went from broke to booked. From overlooked to overexposed.

This is how you dominate the digital world without breaking the bank.

Chapter 4: Conversation is the New Code

Most people think search engines are looking at your website. And they are—kind of. But what they're really looking at is what the rest of the internet is saying about you.

Let me say it clearly: in today's online world, **conversation is more powerful than code.**

You could have the cleanest website in the world—optimized images, fast load speed, perfect tags—and still get beat out by a competitor who's messy but popular. Because search engines are no longer just ranking pages... they're reading the room.

If your name keeps popping up in conversations that are relevant to what people are searching, that carries more weight than any title tag ever could.

Digital Chatter Is the New SEO Signal

The algorithm is paying attention to:

- What people are saying in YouTube comments

- What shows up in Reddit threads

- What reviews say on Google, Yelp, Amazon, or TripAdvisor

- Who's tagging you on TikTok or Instagram

- How often your content gets saved, shared, or stitched

This is what I call **digital chatter**. It's the unstructured, unpredictable, organic signal that tells the algorithm: this person or business is active, relevant, and part of the conversation.

And here's the kicker—it doesn't have to be coming from you.

You can have other people talking about your brand and the algorithm still credits it. In fact, that's even better. It looks more authentic. A dozen people recommending your business in Facebook comments carries more weight than a thousand keywords stuffed onto your About page.

You Don't Need to Go Viral—You Need to Be Mentioned

Most people think the only way to get noticed is to "go viral." That's not true. Virality is a spike. But mentions? Those are momentum.

You want to be:

- Tagged in posts that relate to your niche

- Mentioned in blogs, podcasts, and reviews

- Shared in group chats and DMs

- Commented on in forums and threads

- Quoted, reposted, and referenced

This is how you build what I call **conversational authority**. It means the algorithm sees your name (or brand) come up enough times in enough relevant places that it starts associating you with that topic.

And that's how you win in today's SEO.

Linkless Mentions > Backlinks

Back in the day, SEO was all about backlinks—getting other sites to link to yours. And yes, links still matter. But now there's something just as powerful: **linkless mentions.**

Search engines can now track when your name, brand, or product is mentioned—even if there's no clickable link.

That's huge.

Because now, someone can talk about you in a comment, a video, or a text post and it still strengthens your authority signal.

You could have:

- No website

- No backlinks

- No ad budget

But if 20 different people are talking about your product across platforms? You're going to show up in search.

Conversation Clusters = Visibility Boost

The algorithm doesn't just notice one mention. It looks for **clusters**—patterns of people talking about the same thing, across multiple platforms, in a similar context.

That's why you want to repurpose your content. One blog post becomes a video. That video gets clipped into a short. That short gets stitched. Someone quotes it in a Facebook Group. Someone else links it in Reddit. Before you know it, you've created a cluster—and the algorithm sees that as a signal that you're worth ranking.

This is the **saturation strategy** I've been talking about.

You don't need to rank #1. You need to be everywhere the conversation is happening.

Because when people search—and especially when they use voice assistants—they're not just looking for the answer. They're looking for the name that's already showing up in all the places they trust.

The Internet is a Reputation Game

And here's the truth most marketers avoid: search engines are now building a version of your **reputation** behind the scenes.

They're scoring you based on:

- How often you're mentioned

- Where those mentions come from

- Whether people engage with your name

- Whether people bounce after seeing your stuff

- Whether you're part of the pattern or just a page on the side

This is why SEO isn't just technical anymore. **It's reputational.**

And reputation comes from conversation.

Chapter 5: The Authority Triangle – Visibility, Trust, Relevance

If you've ever wondered what separates the brands that show up online from the ones that don't—it comes down to three things:

Visibility. Trust. Relevance.

I call this the **Authority Triangle**, and it's how search engines decide who deserves to be seen. Not who has the prettiest website. Not who spent the most on ads. Not who hired the fanciest SEO firm.

They want to know three things:

- Are people seeing you? (**Visibility**)

- Do they trust what they see? (**Trust**)

- Is it what they were looking for? (**Relevance**)

Get all three right—and you'll dominate.

---

1. Visibility: Are You Even on the Radar?

You can't get ranked if you don't show up. Period.

Visibility means you're present in all the places that matter:

- Google Business profile

- Social platforms

- Niche forums and groups

- Video platforms like YouTube or TikTok

- Review sites like Yelp, Trustpilot, or Google Reviews

This doesn't mean you have to be viral. It just means you have to **exist—and be discoverable—in more than one place.**

Most businesses put all their effort into their website and wonder why no one finds them. But the algorithm is looking beyond your site. It wants to see if you're part of the bigger picture.

---

2. Trust: Are You Who You Say You Are?

Trust is the second leg of the triangle, and it's where most people fall short.

Search engines look for signs that other people believe you're legit. That includes:

- Reviews (especially consistent ones across platforms)

- Third-party mentions

- Consistent NAP (Name, Address, Phone) data

- Verified profiles

- Backlinks from reputable sites

But it also includes the **tone** of your content.

Does your site sound like it was written by a human or a bot?

Does it answer real questions or just stuff in keywords?

Does it feel sketchy—or solid?

And remember: the algorithm can read tone now. It can tell if something was written to help people—or just to try and rank. That's the difference between **gaming the system** and **working with the system.**

---

3. Relevance: Are You Actually What They Wanted?

Relevance is the dealbreaker. You could be visible. You could be trusted. But if your content doesn't match what someone is actually looking for? You're getting skipped.

Relevance today means:

- Matching search intent (not just search terms)

- Answering the question people meant to ask

- Structuring your content clearly

- Using titles and descriptions that make sense to real people

- Including supporting content like FAQs, comparisons, or demos

This is why structured data and long-tail content clusters work so well. You're giving search engines context—and giving users what they want.

Putting It All Together

Let me give you a real-world comparison.

Imagine someone is looking for a great barbecue joint in Atlanta.

Visibility: You've got a Google Business profile, some YouTube shorts, and a few Instagram reels showing ribs on the smoker. People can find you.

Trust: You've got hundreds of 4–5 star reviews. A local food blogger shouted you out. There's a photo of Killer Mike eating your brisket. That builds trust.

Relevance: Your website clearly says "best BBQ in Atlanta." You have a blog post titled "Why Our Ribs Sell Out by

3PM." You're not trying to rank for tacos or sushi. You're in the right lane.

Now imagine your competitor:
A beautiful, modern website—but no reviews, no social presence, and generic copy like "we serve food you'll love."

Who do you think shows up in the algorithm's top picks?

The Triangle Is Your Blueprint

You don't need to game the system.
You just need to feed it the right signals.

If you're weak in any one corner of the triangle, your visibility suffers. But if you hit all three—visibility, trust, and relevance—the algorithm has every reason to push you to the top.

And here's the good news: you don't need to be the biggest.
You just need to be the most **aligned.**

In the next chapter, I'll show you why that matters even more in the era of voice search—and how to become the one answer that Alexa or Siri gives when someone asks a question.

Because in a voice-first world, only **one** brand gets picked.

Let's make it yours.

Chapter 6: Voice Search and the One-Answer World

Remember when people used to type questions into Google? That still happens—but it's no longer the default. These days, people just ask:

"Hey Siri, where's the best Jamaican food near me?"
"Alexa, what's the best SUV under $30,000?"
"Google, who sells the best hiking boots in Tampa?"

And you know what all those assistants have in common?
They only give one answer.

Not ten links. Not a list of options. **One.**

So if you're not that answer, you don't exist.

Search Is Now a Conversation. And You're Not In It Yet.

The same tracking and conversational patterning we talked about before? That's exactly what drives voice search.

Your phone isn't pulling results from the top of the Google homepage anymore. It's pulling them from **intent clusters**— based on:

- What similar people are asking

- What content is being cited or mentioned the most

- Which brand looks like the best match for that intent

So the only way to become the answer… is to look like the most **trusted**, **most visible**, and **most discussed** result in that niche.

Voice Assistants Pull from Conversations, Not Just Sites

Want to know what Alexa, Siri, and Google Assistant are really doing?

They're aggregating signals from all over the web. That includes:

- Google Business listings
- Reviews
- Blog posts

- Social media chatter

- YouTube content

- Product databases

- Answer forums like Quora or Reddit

- Local directory data

If your business or brand is present in multiple places, talked about by real people, and clearly connected to the question being asked—you get picked. And if you're invisible or generic? You get skipped.

Optimizing for Voice Search Is About One Thing: Trust Clustering

To win in the one-answer world, you have to look like the most natural conclusion.

You can't game your way in. You have to earn your way in—by showing up in enough credible conversations that the algorithm says, "Yep, this must be the one."

That means:

- Building out specific content that answers specific questions

- Making sure your business is listed accurately across all platforms

- Getting reviews that include relevant keywords and phrases

- Getting quoted, reposted, tagged, and embedded in other content

- Structuring your data in ways AI can read (like FAQs, headings, and natural language)

You're not just showing up on a page anymore.
You're showing up in the answer slot.

This Is Why the Old SEO Playbook Fails

The people still obsessing over keyword density and page speed have no idea why they're not showing up on Siri. Because Siri isn't ranking pages.

She's ranking **entities**.

She's looking for the person or business that has:

- A presence in the right categories

- A footprint that matches the question

- A trail of trust across platforms

She's looking for a pattern that feels like the answer—not a website that just says the words.

How to Become the One Answer

If you want to dominate voice search, here's the formula:

Create Answer-Style Content.

- Use natural questions as titles.

- Write in a way that sounds like how people actually speak.

- Use subheadings and bullet points to make it easy for AI to extract.

Get Mentioned on Other Sites.

- Not just backlinks—get your brand into other people's sentences.

- Guest blogs, podcast features, product reviews, community replies.

Get Reviewed with Context.

- Encourage customers to mention what they searched for and why they chose you.

- "Best massage in downtown Chicago" in a review is gold.

Keep Your Info Consistent Everywhere.

- NAP (Name, Address, Phone) has to match across Google, Yelp, Facebook, and everywhere else.

Dominate the Topic Cluster.

- Create multiple pieces of content around one theme so the algorithm sees you as the best match for that subject.

Don't Just Answer. Be the Answer.

In a voice-first world, search engines aren't looking for the best site.
They're looking for the **best match.**

And that match is made up of trust, repetition, and relevance across multiple platforms—not one page.

This is your opportunity to stop playing defense and start playing offense.

You can't afford to just be in the list anymore.
You have to become **the** answer.
And when you do that, you don't just win clicks—you own the space.

In the next chapter, I'll show you exactly how to do that—without blowing your budget.

We'll talk about how to repurpose your content, saturate your niche, and be everywhere—without being overwhelmed.

Let's go.

Chapter 7: Be Everywhere Without Being Broke

Creating content every day sounds exhausting.
And if you think it means writing a new blog post, filming a YouTube video, and recording a podcast from scratch every single time—yeah, it would be.

But here's the thing:
You don't need more content. You need more placements.

You need **more versions** of your content in **more places**.
That's how you saturate your niche without burning out or breaking your budget.

Stop Thinking Like a Creator. Think Like a Distributor.

Most business owners get stuck in content paralysis because they believe every post needs to be original.
But that's not how the pros do it.

Pros **repurpose**.

One blog becomes a video.
That video gets clipped into shorts.
Those shorts become TikToks and Reels.
The audio becomes a podcast.
The transcript becomes social captions.
The comments become testimonials.

You don't need to create 20 things.
You need to create **one thing well—**
and then spin it into 20 formats.

The Rule of One to Many

Here's the formula I teach my clients:

One idea → multiple formats → multiple platforms → massive visibility

Let's say you record a short video explaining "How to start an LLC in Florida for under $100."
Here's how you turn that into saturation:

1. **YouTube Video** – Full explanation, titled with the search question.

2. **Blog Post** – Written version of your explanation, with your own insights added.

3. **Instagram Reel / TikTok** – A 60-second clip of the most actionable tip.

4. **Facebook Post** – Pull a quote or headline from your blog and post it with a link.

5. **LinkedIn Post** – Reword your blog into a first-person business tip post.

6. **Twitter/X Thread** – Break the steps into 5 tweets.

7. **Pinterest Pin** – Create an infographic version of your blog with a free template.

8. **Podcast Clip** – Strip the audio from your video and post it.

Same info. Different outfits.

And the algorithm sees it as 8 separate signals about your expertise.

But Won't That Look Repetitive?

Not to your audience—and definitely not to the algorithm.

Different people live on different platforms.
They like different formats.
They check in at different times of day.

And even if someone sees your message more than once? That's good.
Repetition builds recognition.
Repetition builds trust.
Repetition makes you look like a leader.

You're not annoying them.

You're branding yourself.

Use Tools to Make This Easy

Here's a short stack of tools I personally recommend:

- **Adobe Express** – Free tool to post across all social platforms at once.

- **Canva Pro** – Turn blog quotes into graphics in minutes.

- **Otter.ai or Descript** – Transcribe your videos automatically.

- **Repurpose.io** – Auto-publish your videos to multiple platforms.

- **CapCut or Clipchamp** – Quick mobile video editing with captions and split screens.

If you're doing everything manually, you'll burn out.
Use tools that multiply your reach without multiplying your time.

You Don't Need to Go Viral. You Need to Be Everywhere.

Most business owners are chasing a spike—a viral post, a trending clip, a Hail Mary.

But virality fades.
Presence sticks.

Being present means:

- You're easy to find on every platform

- Your name comes up in every format

- You always look like you're active, trusted, and part of the conversation

That's what builds **saturation**.
And saturation wins.

Create Once. Distribute Endlessly.

Start thinking of your content like seeds.
You don't grow a tree by planting one seed and hoping.
You plant the same seed **in different soil**, **at different angles**, **in different seasons**.

Same message.

Different format.

Different audience.

Different reach.

That's how you saturate.

Summary: The Repurpose Game Plan

1. **Pick a question your audience is asking**

2. **Create a piece of content that answers it clearly**

3. **Turn it into at least 5 different formats**

4. **Post on at least 4 different platforms**

5. **Automate what you can, track what matters, and keep showing up**

In the next chapter, I'll show you how this daily system creates **search dominance** over time—without ever chasing rankings.

We're not here to win the #1 spot.

We're here to own the whole page.

Let's go.

Chapter 8: Own the First Five Pages

Ranking #1 on Google is dead.
And keyword stuffing? That's a fossil
from the 2010s.

In the AI-driven internet, showing up
once doesn't cut it.
What wins now is **presence**—
consistent, trustworthy, embedded
visibility across platforms, formats, and
conversations.
The new search engine isn't just looking
for websites that mention the right
words—it's looking for **authority**,
relevance, and **answers**.

Let's be clear:

AI doesn't rank keyword matches.
It ranks **solutions**.

When someone types in—or speaks—a question, the algorithm scrapes everything it knows about that topic. Not just your title tag. Not just your blog post. It pulls context from:

- Video transcripts

- Blog summaries

- User comments

- Shares

- Reviews

- Product descriptions

- Social chatter

- Public data

It builds a map of **who's talking about the topic** and whether they seem to actually know what they're talking about.

If your name, brand, or business is part of the conversation—**over and over again**, across trusted domains—you win.

Be the Expert. Answer the Questions.

Don't focus on keywords.
Focus on **questions real people ask**.

If you want to show up when someone searches for "how to file taxes as an LLC in Florida," then don't write an article titled "LLC Tax Help."
Write a blog post that actually walks through the forms.

Film a video that shows your screen.
Talk like a human and explain the
process.

Why?
Because Google's AI is trying to
interpret content like a human. It's trying
to determine:

- Does this page actually answer
  the question?

- Does it match the intent behind
  the search?

- Is this source being referenced
  elsewhere?

- Do other trusted pages point back
  to it?

If the answer is yes—it floats to the top.
Not because it's "optimized," but
because it's **helpful**.

How to Actually Do This – The Real-World System I Use

Here's exactly what I do.
No fluff. No theory. Just what works.

1. Set up Adobe Express (it's free)

Connect your Facebook, Instagram, X
(Twitter), and LinkedIn accounts.
This gives you one place to manage
your daily posts across all platforms.
No excuses, no logging in and out of a
dozen apps. This is your daily control
panel.

2. Every day, post a blog based on a long-tail keyword

But not just any keyword. I mean the kind of phrase someone actually searches when they have a problem:

- "How to register a new LLC in Georgia for under $100"

- "What permits do I need to start a food truck in Tampa?"

These are **questions**—not just topics. Write a short blog post answering that one specific question.
Keep it clean. Make sure the keyword is naturally in the text, especially in the headline and first paragraph.

3. Record a video saying the same thing

Doesn't need to be fancy. Just you explaining the same info from the blog. Post it on YouTube. Use the same keyword in your title and description.

Important:

- In your YouTube video description, paste the link to your blog post.

- Then embed the YouTube video into the blog itself.

Now you've created a loop.
The blog drives to the video, and the video drives to the blog.

4. Use Adobe Express to push that blog post to your socials

Open Adobe Express, upload a relevant photo, and post to all four platforms with the blog link.

Do this every day.

You've now turned one piece of content into five:

- A blog post

- A YouTube video

- Four social shares

- And it all points back to your site

5. Want to go even harder? Upload the same video to Vimeo

Use a different title. Write a fresh description.

You've now got another property helping

your content show up in search—without writing a single extra word.

Do this with:

- Blogs (also post them on Medium or LinkedIn)

- Reviews (ask clients to leave keyword-rich reviews across platforms)

- Brand mentions (get quoted in forums, interviews, press releases, etc.)

The more properties you can find to share on, the more you dominate search presence online.

Why This Works

Because you begin to **show up everywhere**.

To Google, you're not a one-hit wonder.
You're a consistent voice.
You're answering real questions.
And your name keeps popping up—on your site, on YouTube, on Facebook, on LinkedIn, even on Vimeo.

You're not chasing rankings.
You're building **presence**.

Think of It This Way…

When you go to search for something, who do you trust more?

- Someone who shows up once, no matter how polished the result is?

- Or someone who covers the first five pages—in articles, in videos, in reviews, on maps, in image results?

That's not a fluke.
That's **saturation**.

That's how the algorithm thinks:
Who keeps showing up?
And that's how people think too:
Who looks legit?

You're not hoping to get picked.
You're flooding the space until you are the **obvious answer**.

In the next chapter, I'll show you how to **protect the visibility** you've earned—

so one algorithm update doesn't wipe you out.

Because owning the first five pages is just the beginning.

You've got to hold the ground you earned.

Chapter 9: Algorithm-Proof Your Business

Most people treat SEO like a one-time project.
They tweak their website, post a blog or two, maybe hire someone to fix their meta tags… and then they wait.
And wait.
And wonder why nothing happens.

Here's the truth:
SEO isn't a goal. It's a momentum game.

Once the algorithm starts noticing you—once you begin to show up in conversations, on platforms, in search queries—you can't stop.
Because if you do? You fall off the radar just as fast as you got on it.

This is why metrics like "ranking position" or "bounce rate" don't tell the full story.

What really matters is:

Are people still talking about you?
Are you still being seen, shared, and referenced?

If not, you're losing momentum.

Visibility Is a Living Signal

Google doesn't want to rank ghosts.
It wants to rank **active**, **trustworthy**, **current** sources.

You might've had a great blog post six months ago.
But if no one's interacted with it lately, it fades.

Worse—if your competitors are publishing newer, more helpful content, they take your place.

That's why you need to feed the machine **constantly**:

- Keep posting updated content

- Keep joining niche conversations

- Keep encouraging reviews, comments, shares, and saves

- Keep cross-posting to multiple platforms

Think of SEO like fire.
You don't build it once and walk away.
You **keep feeding it**—or it goes out.

Don't Watch Numbers—Watch Signals

Most business owners obsess over the wrong metrics:

- Website traffic

- Keyword rankings

- Bounce rate

- Domain authority

None of those tell you if people are **talking about you**.

What you want to track is:

- **Mentions** – Are you being talked about in forums, threads, reviews, and posts?

- **Shares** – Is your content being shared, stitched, or referenced?

- **Search queries** – Are people typing in your name or brand, not just generic terms?

- **Engagement** – Are people actually responding to your presence?

Momentum is about **motion**. If you're part of the ongoing conversation, you're winning—even if your "position" doesn't say #1.

How to Build Enduring Momentum

Here's what I recommend to keep your name alive in the algorithm's brain:

1. Repurpose everything

Don't just post once. Turn every idea into multiple formats:

- Blog

- Video

- Podcast quote

- Carousel post

- YouTube Short

- Reddit answer

- TikTok explainer

Spread the same message **everywhere**. That repetition is what reinforces your signal.

2. Schedule mentions

Every week, make it a goal to:

- Get tagged in a group or forum

- Be quoted in a relevant thread

- Publish or comment on something valuable

- Share a fresh take on an old topic

This isn't passive.

You're **fueling visibility** manually—until it snowballs on its own.

3. Monitor your name like a brand

Use tools like:

- Google Alerts

- BrandMentions

- Talkwalker

- Mention.com

Set up alerts for your name, your business, and your core services.
You want to see where and how you're showing up.

If you're not showing up at all? That's a signal to **get louder**.

The Plateau Isn't the Problem— Stopping Is

Most brands hit a point where growth slows.
That's not failure—that's your next phase.
What kills momentum is **stopping**.

The algorithm assumes silence means irrelevance.

So if you don't keep showing up,
someone else will take your spot.

Don't fall for the illusion that visibility
"sticks" just because you earned it once.
It doesn't.
It needs **nurturing**.

You Don't Need Viral—You Need Volume

You don't need one big win.
You need lots of little signals.

Think of it like digital gravity.
Every comment, post, or tag adds
weight to your presence.
Eventually, the algorithm can't ignore
you—even if you never "go viral."

Because what it sees is someone **consistently part of the conversation.**

That's what wins.

Keep the Fire Lit

Here's your weekly checklist:

- ☑ Answer 1 real question in a blog
- ☑ Film 1 video explaining the same thing
- ☑ Post across 4 platforms
- ☑ Leave 2 comments in relevant groups
- ☑ Ask for 1 review or mention
- ☑ Track your name for changes in visibility

Do that, every week, and you'll **never fall off the map**.

This is how real brands build unshakable visibility.

Not with tricks.

Not with rank-chasing.

But with **momentum**.

Chapter 10: The Invisible Funnel

If your online presence isn't creating customers, you don't have a funnel— you have a dead end.

Most people think of sales funnels like this:

1. Run an ad

2. Capture an email

3. Send a drip campaign

4. Sell something

That's not how today's world works. Consumers are smarter. Ad fatigue is real. And email open rates are in the toilet. What actually works is building trust before they even realize they're in a funnel.

That's what I call the **Invisible Funnel**.

You're Being Researched Without Knowing It

Here's what people actually do before they buy:

- They Google you

- They read your reviews

- They skim your blog

- They stalk your social media

- They check to see if other people trust you

And they do all of that before they ever give you their email address—let alone their money.

If your digital footprint isn't designed to move them forward, you've already lost the sale.

Visibility Builds Trust Without Pitching

In the invisible funnel, the sale begins before you ever say a word.

Every post, every comment, every video you make is a breadcrumb.

- Someone sees your blog and thinks: "Smart."

- They catch your name again on YouTube: "Familiar."

- A Reddit thread mentions your business: "Trusted."

- They find your Google profile full of reviews: "Legit."

They haven't opted into anything, but you've already moved them closer.

This is passive conversion. And it works.

The 5 Layers of an Invisible Funnel

1. **Search Visibility**
   You show up when they Google a question.

2. **Content Authority**
   You've got helpful content that matches the problem they have.

3. **Third-Party Proof**
   Other people are talking about you (reviews, forums, interviews).

4. **Platform Presence**

   You're active where they hang out—LinkedIn, YouTube, Instagram, TikTok.

5. **Offer Access**

   When they finally click "Contact" or "Buy," it doesn't feel like a leap. It feels obvious.

Real Funnels Don't Feel Like Funnels

If your funnel feels pushy, you're doing it wrong.

People want to feel like they found you—not like they were chased.

The best funnel is invisible because it feels like their idea:

- "I saw your video."

- "Someone mentioned your name."

- "I kept seeing your stuff everywhere."

That's the moment you win. Not because of a clever ad. But because you saturated the conversation and built trust before the pitch.

Create Pathways, Not Pipelines

Instead of thinking like a traditional marketer, think like a guide.

Your job is to:

- Be findable when they're curious

- Be helpful when they're unsure

- Be visible when they're comparing

- Be the obvious choice when they're ready

That's how you game the system.

And in the final chapter, I'll show you exactly how to keep this momentum going—so you stay relevant, present, and profitable no matter what the algorithm throws at you next.

Chapter 11: Final Thoughts – Master the Game, Don't Chase It

By now, you've seen the pattern.

Visibility isn't magic—it's momentum. And the businesses that win online aren't necessarily the best... they're the most **present**, **talked about**, and **trusted** in the right spaces.

You don't need to be a tech expert. You don't need a big ad budget. You don't even need to rank #1 on Google.

You just need to **be visible where it counts**.

That means showing up in conversations that matter.
That means building **real authority**, not rented reach.

That means making content that answers **actual questions**, not just chasing keywords.

Stop Reacting. Start Saturating.

The old SEO game was reactive:
Wait for rankings to drop → scramble to fix it.

But the winners now are proactive.
They **flood the space** with valuable content before the algorithm even shifts.
They build trust before the pitch.
They don't try to out-hack Google—they **align with it**.

This book was never about tricks. It was about **strategy**.

Because the people who master visibility don't chase clicks—they **command attention**.

Your Final Checklist

Here's what to do next—whether you're starting from scratch or reinventing yourself:

☑ **Google yourself** monthly
Check what shows up on pages 1–5. Own your name. Own your niche.

☑ **Answer real questions**
Use tools like AnswerThePublic or look at your DMs. What are people actually asking?

☑ Publish daily content

Short or long. Doesn't matter. Just be consistent.

☑ Repurpose like a machine

One blog = one video = four social posts = one newsletter = a podcast clip. Stretch it.

☑ Build conversational authority

Get mentioned, tagged, reviewed. Show up in comments. Be where people talk.

☑ Use the triangle

Every piece of content should build **visibility**, earn **trust**, and deliver **relevance**.

☑ Dominate the first five pages

Not by ranking #1, but by **saturating**

with helpful, branded content across platforms.

✅ Track momentum, not vanity

Forget page views. Watch for shares, saves, mentions, and referrals.

If You're Just Starting Now...

Here's your 5-day launch plan:

Day 1: Claim your name. Set up Google Business, social profiles, and a basic website.

Day 2: Write a blog post answering one specific question.

Day 3: Record a 60-second video explaining that post. Upload to YouTube.

Day 4: Post the blog and video link

across every platform.

Day 5: Ask a friend or customer to leave a review or mention you somewhere trusted.

Repeat that for 4 weeks, and you'll already be ahead of 90% of small businesses.

Final Words

The system isn't rigged. It's just misunderstood.

It doesn't reward the loudest. It rewards the most **present**, **consistent**, and **useful**.

That can be you.

One of the most important things is to do proper keyword research. Real Keywords Should have decent traffic but low competition. Reach out to me if you need help with that. Then use that #keyword EVERYWHERE!

Make sure that you're posting several times a day and have google analytics on your websites.

Stop chasing the game.
Master it.
Show up where people search.
Say something that matters.
And let the algorithm work for you—not the other way around.

The future belongs to the **visible**.
And you're ready.

How Do You Know It's Working?

If you pick proper keyword phrases, and post and cross-post every day as I've described—using real-world context in real-world blogs, videos, and social media—and you **cross-link and cross-share** that content across platforms, you should start seeing results in Google within **six weeks**.

If you're not seeing traction by then, reach out to me. We'll figure out what's missing and **tighten it up**.

But whatever you do—**save the ad budget** for people who don't know what to do with their money.

www.ingramcontent.com/pod-product-compliance
Lightning Source LLC
Chambersburg PA
CBHW030527210326
41597CB00013B/1056